Grandmother
Remembers

Grandmother Remembers

A Written Heirloom for My Grandchild

Conceived and written by Judith Levy
Designed and illustrated by Judy Pelikan

A Welcome Book

Stewart, Tabori & Chang, Publishers, New York

Edited by Marya Dalrymple

Text copyright © 1983 by Judith Levy
Illustrations copyright © 1983 by Pelikan Inc.

34th Printing

Published in 1983 by Stewart, Tabori & Chang, Publishers, Inc., New York.

Distributed in the U.S. by Workman Publishing,
708 Broadway, New York, New York 10003
Distributed in Canada by Canadian Manda Group,
P.O. Box 920 Station U, Toronto, Ontario M8Z 5P9

Printed and bound in Hong Kong

I offer you my memories
So that you will know
Your Grandmother was a little girl
Not so long ago.

With love for _____

From _____

Date _____

Table of Contents

"Grandmother" Around the World

I like to be called _____

Afrikaans: Ouma
Arabic: Sitt
Bulgarian: Baba
Chinese: Zu-mu
Danish: Farmor, Mormor
Dutch: Oma
English: Grandmother
    Grandma
    Grandmama
    Granny
    Nana
    Nanny
Eskimo: Aana, Maurluq
Finnish: Isoäiti, Mummi
French: Grand-mère
German: Grossmutter
Greek: Yiayia
Hawaiian: Kupuna wahine, Tutu

Hebrew: Savta
Hungarian: Nagyanana
Irish: Mama, Seanmháthair
Italian: Nonna
Japanese: Oba-San
Korean: Hal Mo-ni
Norwegian: Farmor, Mormor
Polish: Babcia
Portuguese: Avó
Romanian: Bunica
Russian: Babushka
Spanish: Abuela, Abuelita
Swahili: Nyanya
Swedish: Farmor, Mormor
Turkish: Büyük anne
Vietnamese: Bà
Welsh: Mam-gu, Nain
Yiddish: Bobe
Zulu: Ukhulu, Isalukazi

Our Family Tree

You, my little apple,
Sprang from a sturdy tree.
Branches of generations
Embrace you tenderly.

Great Grandmother

Great Grandmother

Great Grandmother

Great Grandfather

Great Grandfather

Great Grandmother

Great Grandfather

Great Grandfather

Grandfather

Grandmother

Grandfather

Grandmother

Mother

Father

Name

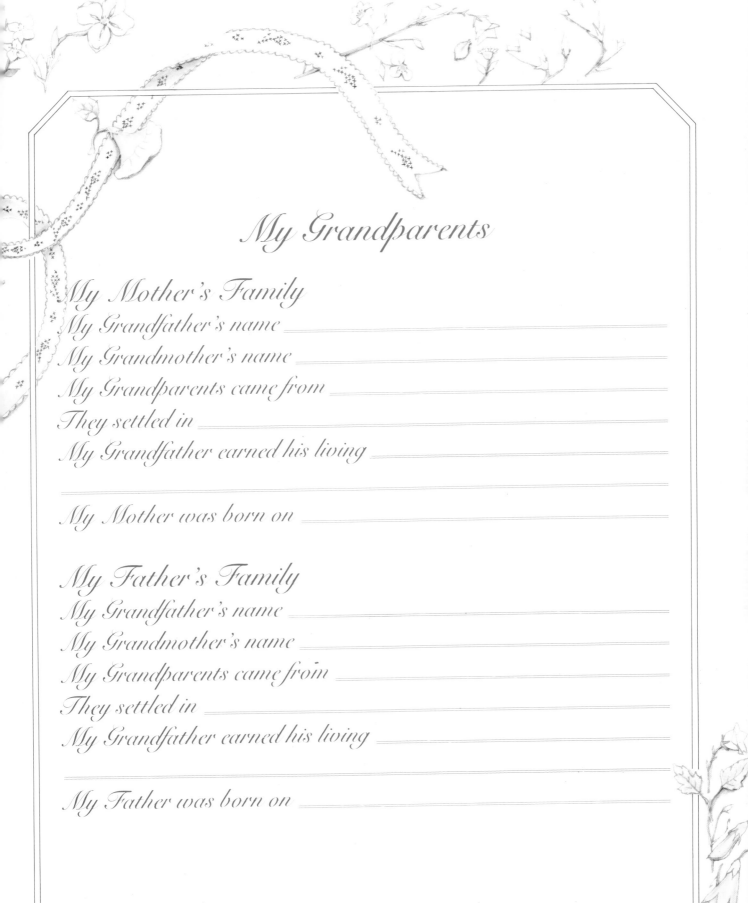

My Grandparents

My Mother's Family
My Grandfather's name _____
My Grandmother's name _____
My Grandparents came from _____
They settled in _____
My Grandfather earned his living _____
_____

My Mother was born on _____

My Father's Family
My Grandfather's name _____
My Grandmother's name _____
My Grandparents came from _____
They settled in _____
My Grandfather earned his living _____
_____

My Father was born on _____

*Photograph of
Grandmother's Parents*

My Parents

The dearest friends in life
A little girl ever had
Were the two special people
I called "Mom" and "Dad."

My Father's name _____

My Mother's name _____

My parents met

　How _____

_____

_____

　When _____

_____

　Where _____

_____

They were married

　Date _____

　Place _____

My Father earned his living _____

_____

Photograph of
Grandmother as a Baby

I Was Born

About the day that I was born
There's much that I don't know.
But here are just a few facts
My Mother said were so.

I was born

    When _____

    Where _____

I was named _____

That name was chosen because _____

_____

_____

I weighed _____

I was told I resembled _____

_____

My brothers' and sisters' names _____

_____

Photograph of
Grandmother
as a Young Girl

As a Young Girl

Life is like a rosebud
Waiting to unfold.
Each petal is a story
Waiting to be told.

My family lived _____

_____

I went to school _____

_____

As a student I _____

_____

My ambition was _____

_____

_____

At home I was expected to _____

_____

My parents were very strict about _____

_____

_____

My Father taught me to value _____
_____

My Mother taught me to value _____
_____

What I loved most about my Father was _____
_____

What I loved most about my Mother was _____
_____

My teenage years were _____
_____
_____

As a Girl "My Favorite…"

Song _____

Movie _____

Actor _____

Actress _____

Book _____

Radio program _____

Season _____

Vacation spot _____

Holiday _____

Flower _____

Color _____

Sport _____

Food _____

Subject in school _____

Friend _____

As a Young Woman

I was graduated from _____

    Date _____

After I finished school I _____

_____

I worked as _____

_____

On weekends I _____

_____

The fashion rage at the time was _____

_____

_____

I started to date at the age of _____

I met your Grandfather at _____

_____

His full name _____

His birthday _____

His heritage _____

Our first date was _____

_____

_____

His age when we met was _____

He lived _____

I lived _____

He earned his living _____

_____

I liked him because _____

_____

_____

Grandfather said he liked me because _____

_____

_____

When we dated we liked to go _____

_____

_____

My Engagement

Photograph of
the
Engaged Couple

Of all the men in the world
I knew he was the best,
So when Grandfather asked to marry me,
I happily said, "Yes!"

Our courtship lasted _____

When I told my parents they _____

_____

We became engaged on _____

When Grandfather proposed he said _____

_____

_____

*Photograph of
Grandmother as a Bride*

My Wedding Day

I put my hand in his hand,
As we stood side by side,
On that very special day
When I became a bride.

Grandfather and I were married

Date _____

Time _____

Place _____

I wore _____

We celebrated our wedding by _____

_____

_____

Our most memorable wedding gift was _____

_____

My most vivid memory of my wedding day is _____

_____

_____

After we married we traveled to _____

_____

Photograph of
Grandmother
and Grandfather
as a
Young Couple

My First Year of Marriage

When Grandfather and I were first married we lived in _____

_____

_____

We lived there for _____

My fondest memory of our first home is _____

_____

_____

_____

Grandfather's job was _____

_____

After we married I _____

_____

_____

When we took trips, we liked to go _____

_____

_____

As a wife I tried to be _____

_____

_____

_____

Photograph of
Grandmother and Baby

Your Parent Was Born

The day I had a baby
Surely changed my life.
We were now a family;
I was a Mother and a Wife.

Your parent was born
   When _____
   Where _____
   We lived at _____
Full name _____
We chose that name because _____
_____

Color of eyes at birth _____
Color of hair at birth _____
Weight at birth _____
I thought my baby resembled _____
Brothers' and sisters' names _____
_____

Favorite toy was _____
First word was _____
Sometimes we used the nickname _____
I still smile when I think about the time _____
_____
_____

*Photograph of
Grandmother and
Young Child*

My Child Growing Up

The growing years were busy,
Speeding swiftly by.
A decade went past
In the blinking of an eye.

Schools attended were _____

_____

_____

Best subject in school was _____

_____

_____

Showed talent in _____

_____

_____

Ambition was _____

_____

_____

Hobbies were _____

_____

My Child's Teenage Years

Favorite type of music was _____

_____

Favorite sport was _____

Major interests were _____

_____

_____

Household duties were _____

_____

Spare time was spent _____

_____

_____

Dating began at the age of _____

I set a curfew of _____

I was strict about _____

_____

_____

I was very proud that _____

_____

What I remember most about those teenage years is _____

_____

_____

_____

Photograph of Teenager

*Photograph of
the Young Couple*

Your Parents

They Met

How _____

_____

_____

_____

When _____

Where _____

_____

_____

They Were Married

Date _____

Place _____

_____

*Photograph of
Grandchild as a Baby*

Your Birth

The day you were born
All my dreams came true.
I'm the proudest Grandmother
To have a Grandchild like you.

You were born

When _____

Where _____

When I first heard the news I _____

_____

I thought you resembled _____

_____

When I brag about you I always say _____

_____

_____

When Our Family Gets Together

*Heritage is more precious
With every passing day.
Traditions keep us close,
In a very special way.*

We always recall the time _____

_____

_____

We fondly laugh about _____

_____

_____

We still remember when you _____

_____

_____

_____

I am happy that we all _____

_____

_____

_____

_____

I think our family is special because _____

_____

_____

The first holiday you shared with us was _____

_____

Photograph of Our Family

Holiday Traditions

Holiday _____

Date or season _____

We celebrate this holiday by _____

_____

_____

The special foods served are _____

_____

Holiday _____

Date or season _____

We celebrate this holiday by _____

_____

_____

The special foods served are _____

_____

Holiday _____

Date or season _____

We celebrate this holiday by _____

_____

_____

The special foods served are _____

_____

Holiday _____

Date or season _____

We celebrate this holiday by _____

_____

_____

The special foods served are _____

_____

Family Recipes

Grandmother taught my mother
And my mother taught me
These delicious family recipes
I offer lovingly.

A Family Favorite _____

Ingredients and Directions _____

_____

_____

_____

_____

_____

_____

_____

_____

_____

_____

_____

_____

_____

_____

_____

A Family Favorite _____

Ingredients and Directions _____

A Family Favorite _____

Ingredients and Directions _____

Dear Relatives

I'd like to help identify
So it's really clear,
Some members of our family
Who are so very dear.

Name

Relationship

Photograph

Name

Relationship

Photograph

Name

Relationship

Photograph

Name

Relationship

Photograph

*Photograph of
Grandmother Today*

I was naughty when I was little,
I got into mischief too,
But my Grandmother always loved me,
And I'll always love you.

Thoughts I'd Like to Share with You

Because you are so dear to me,
To you I will reveal
Special thoughts, from my heart,
Of how I truly feel.

My deepest values are _____
_____
_____

I was proud of _____
_____
_____
_____

Everyone thought I shouldn't, but I was glad I _____
_____
_____
_____

I was in for a complete surprise when _____

_____

_____

A matter of concern was _____

_____

_____

I was always sorry I didn't _____

_____

_____

I felt very strongly about _____

_____

_____

I've changed my mind, and now I think _____

_____

_____

How the World Has Changed Since
I Was a Little Girl

They invented _____

_____

They discovered _____

_____

They succeeded in preventing _____

_____

When man landed on the moon I _____

_____

A time saver my mother never had is _____

_____

Women today _____

_____

Movies today _____

_____

Dating today is different because _____

_____

_____

I still like the old-fashioned ways of _____

_____

_____

I think the younger generation is wiser about _____

_____

I think a woman president would be _____

_____

Today "My Favorite…"

Song _____

Movie _____

Actor _____

Actress _____

Book _____

Television program _____

Newscaster _____

Season _____

Vacation spot _____

Holiday _____

Flower _____

Color _____

Dessert _____

Saying _____

_____

The Future

Someday you'll have a Grandchild
And you will surely see
Why being your Grandmother
Means the world to me.

My wish for the future is _____

_____

_____

_____

_____

_____

_____

_____

_____

_____

_____

Photograph of Grandfather

Grandfather Would Want You to Know

I Forgot to Mention

Treasures I Have Saved for You

My story would be incomplete
Without these souvenirs.
Precious little keepsakes
I've treasured all these years.